WEIRD, TRUE FACTS

BUGS

Grace Ramsey

Rourke
Educational Media
rourkeeducationalmedia.com

Parts of An Insect

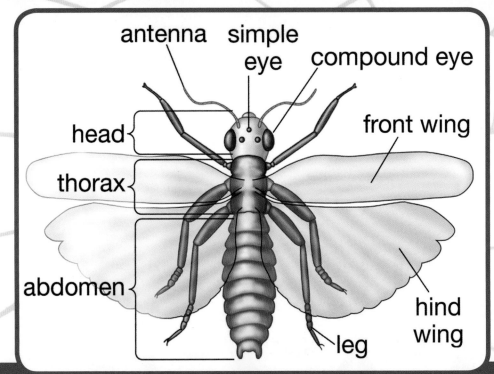

antenna simple eye compound eye front wing head thorax abdomen hind wing leg

Insects have three main body parts: the head, thorax, and abdomen. All insects have six legs. Most have two sets of wings. The wings and legs are attached to the thorax.

A true bug has piercing, straw-like mouth parts called stylets used to suck blood or juices from animals or plants. A true bug's mouthparts are contained in a beak, or proboscis, which may be held under its body when it's not being used. The proboscis of a true bug is not retractable.

Table of Contents

Bugs Versus Insects

Did you know all bugs are insects but not all insects are bugs? Most people use the word *bug* to mean any insect. But scientifically speaking, bugs are only the insects in the order *Hemiptera*. These include cicadas, bed bugs, aphids, assassin bugs, stink bugs, giant water bugs, leafhoppers, and others. There are more than 40 thousand known **species** of true bugs.

The main difference between true bugs and other insects is their mouths. True bugs suck! A true bug has a beak-like mouth that works like a straw. They use it to suck fluids from plants or blood from animals.

An assassin bug nymph explores an oak leaf.

Baby Bugs

Some insects hatch as larvae. True bugs hatch as nymphs, a mini version of the adult bug.

Who Says?

Biologists who name animals and plants are called taxonomists. They decide what's a bug and what's just an insect!

stink bug
proboscis

Weird Bugs

Now that you know the difference, let's check out some weird facts about true bugs!

Assassin Bugs

Assassin bugs are the tiny ninjas of the bug world. They can time their movements to match the blowing of the wind. They use their bodies to mimic the surroundings of their prey. And just when the target realizes it's not a fluttering leaf, it's too late.

An assassin bug can hunt and kill prey twice its size. It uses its venom to paralyze and dissolve the guts of its still-living victim, turning it into a sludge. Slurp! The assassin bug sucks up its meal.

An assassin bug dines on a honey bee.

Once an assassin bug eats its prey, it might stick the empty body on its back with a special sticky fluid. This body armor gives it cover and serves as a protective barrier against predators. Anything that goes after an assassin bug covered in this stuff is going to get a mouthful of **corpses** while the assassin bug escapes!

An assassin bug turns the bodies of its prey into armor.

ambush bug

Ambush bugs tend to be bright colors so they blend into their favorite hiding places: flowers!

An ambush bug is a smaller version of the assassin bug. Like its name suggests, this bug lies in wait for prey to cross its path.

Ambush bugs eat bees, wasps, caterpillars, and flies. Gardeners love them because they eat insects that destroy plants.

A kiss can be sweet, but not when it comes from a kissing bug! Kissing bugs are a type of assassin bug. These creepy critters like to bite people near their mouths while they're sleeping. Eek!

kissing bug

Chagas disease, a potentially life-threatening illness, is spread by kissing bugs. This child's swollen eye and mouth sore were caused by Chagas disease.

The kissing bug also poops after it bites. If the person scratches their face and the poop was infected with a parasite, illness can follow.

Aphids

Most aphids are female. And when they're born, many are already pregnant! This means they can populate an area quite quickly. They feed on plant sap, which is mostly sugar. Know what that means? Yep. They poop sugar. This sweet secretion is called honeydew.

Drop a cookie on the ground and the ants will come. Ants love sugar. That's why some of them adopt aphids. These ants carry aphids from plant to plant. They milk them for honeydew. In exchange, they protect the aphids from predators. In some cases, the ants take the aphids to their nests in the winter to keep them safe until the weather warms.

That's a Lot of Babies!

A single aphid in ideal conditions could produce 600 billion **descendants** in one season.

Some aphid moms give birth to live young. Others lay eggs.

Most aphids are wingless. But if a plant gets too crowded, a generation of winged aphids may be produced so they can relocate.

aphid

winged aphid

Aphids aren't all sweet. They can also be fierce. These tiny fighters kick their pursuers with their hind feet. They may also stab the eggs of their predators to kill their enemies before they hatch.

Stink Bugs

Stink bugs, well, stink! These bugs **emit** a yucky odor when they feel threatened. Or if they're crushed. Some people think they smell like skunks. Others say burnt tires. But stink bugs can produce another smell too: when they find a safe place to hibernate, they send up a smelly invitation for other stink bugs to join them. This smell is undetectable to humans.

Smelly Ladies

Many people love ladybugs. Which, by the way, are insects, not bugs. But these spotted sweeties also stink when they're disturbed or smooshed. The foul odor can linger for hours.

Stink bugs are also called shield bugs.

Stinky and Delicious

Some animals don't mind the stench of stink bugs. Lizards, mice, bluebirds, and ground beetles will happily devour them.

Giant Water Bugs

Giant water bugs are some of the largest true bugs. They are attracted to light, so sometimes they're called electric-light bugs. Like assassin bugs, giant water bugs inject poison that dissolves their prey, then suck up the slush.

To ward off predators, some giant water bugs play dead. Others emit a smelly fluid from their rear-ends.

How does a giant water bug walk on water? Its legs are covered in thousands of microscopic hairs that trap air and increase its buoyancy. Its legs are so buoyant, they can support 15 times the bug's weight!

eggs

A giant water bug can stay afloat in waves and rainstorms.

Look out! The bite of a giant water bug is painful to humans.

eggs

Some female water bugs glue their eggs to the backs of males.

Bed bugs hide for five to ten days after a meal to digest it, mate, and lay eggs.

Bed Bugs

Bed bugs are blood suckers that feast on sleeping humans. Their bite is not painful at first because their saliva acts as an anesthetic. This way their sleeping dinner doesn't wake!

Mmm...Fruity

To some people, bed bugs smell like rotting raspberries. And beagles can be trained to sniff them out!

Bed bugs know how to stay out of sight. They hide in baseboards, mattress crevices, and even picture frames. The carbon dioxide people exhale brings them out of their hiding spots at night.

They can suck blood for up to ten minutes at a time with one stick of their proboscis.

Bed bugs can live for several months between meals. They can also survive extreme cold and heat. And they can live anywhere! This makes them difficult to get rid of.

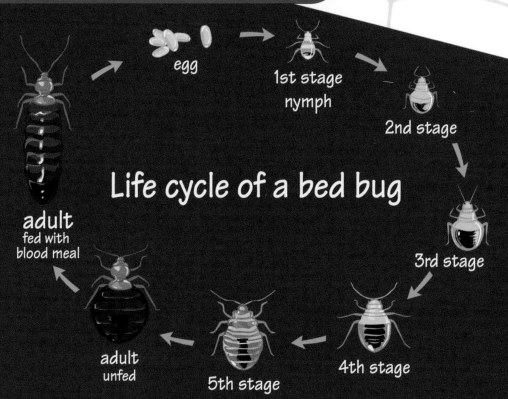

egg

1st stage nymph

2nd stage

Life cycle of a bed bug

adult
fed with
blood meal

3rd stage

adult
unfed

4th stage

5th stage

Bed bugs are ancient pests. Scientists say they may date back 245 thousand years! Scientists think modern humans **evolved** about 200 thousand years ago. That means bed bugs have likely been around longer than we have!

Cicadas

Annual cicadas appear every year. Periodical cicadas only emerge every 13 or 17 years. Adult periodical cicadas cut slits in tree branches to lay their eggs in. When the eggs hatch, the nymphs drop and burrow into the ground. They spend their 13- or 17-year childhoods growing under there! When they're ready to come up, they climb a tree, shed their nymph skin, and emerge as adults.

Cicadas are loud! A swarm of cicadas can produce sounds up to 120 decibels. That's louder than a rock concert! Sometimes cicadas are attracted to people using lawnmowers. The females mistake the sound for singing males—and the males follow.

Loud and Proud

Some cicada songs can be heard up to a mile (1.6 kilometers) away. And every species has its own song.

Periodical cicadas are only found in eastern North America.

Life is Short

Adults only live for four to six weeks. They spend this time mating and avoiding predators. Practically anything will eat a cicada. Even people!

A cicada sheds its skin.

Beyond Bugs: Weird Insect Facts

Old as Dirt

Roaches have been around since the dinosaur days, possibly even before some dinosaurs!

Roaches

Roaches make many people squeamish. But did you know out of thousands of cockroach species, only about 30 types are considered pests? Weird!

Roaches can go up to 40 minutes without breathing. They can survive up to 30 minutes underwater.

There are a lot of myths about roaches. One of the most popular is that the critters can survive nuclear explosions. This isn't true. They can withstand 10 times more radiation than humans, though. Roaches are also thought to only live in dirty homes. False! Roaches will live anywhere they can enter easily and have access to food and water. They are so adaptable, they live on every continent except Antarctica.

Another roach myth is that the wily creepy-crawlies can live without their heads. This is true! Roaches breathe through small holes in their body segments. Since it doesn't need a head to breathe, the headless body can survive for up to a week. It eventually dies of dehydration since it can't drink water.

23

Ants

You know ants live in colonies. But did you know some of those colonies have slaves? Slave-maker ants steal eggs, babies (larvae), and sometimes adults from other nests. The other ants may notice, but scientists say they don't fight back. That's because the slave-makers are fierce! They **wield** their stingers like swords, stabbing ants who dare resist. The captured ants are then brought to the attacking colony's nest to work.

Alternate Strategies

Some slave-maker ants raid a nest, kill the queen and other adults, then wait for the babies to hatch. Those babies will become slave ants.

Experiments have shown some slave-maker ants will die if separated from their slave, even if food is given to them.

Have you ever heard the saying "an army of ants"? It's quite fitting! A swarm of ants does look like an army. But it goes further than that: ants are said to engage in warfare tactics such as tactical deception and strategic placement much like humans.

bulldog ant

World Record Holders

The bulldog ant is the most dangerous on Earth, according to Guinness World Records. This small dangerous ant but mighty Australian biter is responsible for the deaths of three people since 1936. It earned its name with its aggressive, fearless behavior. Fun fact: it can leap seven times the length of its body!

Engineers and architects use termite mounds as inspiration for designing energy-efficient buildings.

Termites

Termites have been around since before the dinosaur days. Scientists think they first appeared on Earth more than 250 million years ago. They are pests to people because they eat the wood in their homes. But termites are vital to the planet! Termite colonies infest dead and dying trees, speeding up the natural **decay**. This lets new growth begin.

Two queen termites surrounded by workers

All Hail the Queen

Termite queens are 30 times the size of the workers. They produce about 30 eggs per minute. And they are a tasty treat for people in Singapore. They are served alive, dipped in alcohol, or preserved in rice wine.

Termites toil around the clock. They never sleep! They are serious about their construction. Termites build the largest structures in the animal kingdom relative to their size. Their mounds can tower 30 feet (9.1 meters) high. Recently scientists discovered that the mound acts like a lung, using chimneys to pull in oxygen and flush out carbon dioxide.

More Really Weird, True Facts About Insects and Bugs

Some honeybee queens quack.

A caterpillar has more muscles than a human. A lot more. A human has more than 650 named muscles. Some species of caterpillars have four thousand.

In 1947, fruit flies became the first living creatures launched into space. Their container parachuted back to Earth. They were recovered alive.

A dung beetle can pull more than a thousand times its weight.

Mosquitoes are attracted to stinky feet! They can detect differences in the way our body parts smell. They figured out they're less likely to get swatted or squashed below our ankles. Clever little blood-suckers! A mosquito is not considered a bug because its proboscis is retractable.

Stoneflies do push-ups.

Crickets detect sound through their knees.

Some ants explode when they're attacked! Exploding ants, also known as Kamikaze ants, have toxic substances in their heads and on the sides of their bodies. When threatened, they explode their heads or rupture their bodies to spew the poison all over their predator. They sacrifice themselves to protect the nest.

Giant water bugs are also called alligator fleas, alligator ticks, and toe-biters.

A praying mantis is the only known insect that can turn its head 180 degrees, an entire half circle.

Glossary

corpses (korps-es): dead bodies

decay (di-KAY): the breaking down of plant or animal matter by natural causes

descendants (di-SEN-duhnts): a person or animal's children, their children, and so on

emit (i-MIT): to produce or send out something such as light, heat, signals, or sound

evolved (i-vahlvd): changed slowly and naturally over time

parasite (PAR-uh-site): an animal or plant that lives on or inside another animal or plant

species (SPEE-seez): one of the groups into which animals and plants of the same genus are divided

wield (weeld): wave around or brandish

Index

Show What You Know

1. What's the difference between a bug and an insect?

2. Which insects build the largest structures in the world relative to their size?

3. How long have bed bugs been on Earth?

4. What do kissing bugs do to humans?

5. How do giant water bugs walk on water?

Further Reading

Honovich, Nancy and Murawski, Darlyne, *Ultimate Bugopedia: The Most Complete Bug Reference Ever*, National Geographic Kids, 2013.

Romero, Libby, *Ultimate Explorer Field Guide: Insects: Find Adventure! Go Outside! Have Fun! Be a Backyard Insect Inspector!*, National Geographic Kids, 2017.

DK, *Everything You Need to Know About Bugs*, DK Children, 2015.

About the Author

Grace Ramsey is fascinated by everything weird and unusual. Her favorite thing about being a writer is learning new things in her research. Grace doesn't like bugs in her house, and she definitely doesn't like to touch them, but she still thinks they're some of the coolest creatures on Earth. Except kissing bugs. Those are just nasty.

Meet The Author!
www.meetREMauthors.com

PHOTO CREDITS: Cover & Title Pg ©arlindo71, ©Ljupco, ©Antagain, ©Serg_Velusceac, ©chengyuzheng, Pgs 2, 3, 4, 5, 7, 8, 10, 11, 13, 15, 17, 18, 19, 20, 21, 22, 23, 24, 25, 28, 29 ©Serg_Velusceac, Pg 2 ©BB4MFB, ©Nigel Cattlin/Alamy Stock Photo, Pg 4 ©Diana Meister/Alamy Stock Photo, ©Goldfinch4ever, Pg 5 ©blickwinkel/Alamy Stock Photo, Pg 6 ©imageBROKER/Alamy Stock Photo, Pg 7 ©Christian Musat/Alamy Stock Photo, Pg 8 ©By Herman Wong HM, Pg 9 ©blickwinkel/Alamy Stock Photo, Pg 10 ©nathanphoto, ©konstantin32, Pg 11 ©CDC/Dr. Mae Melvin [Public domain], Pg 12 ©diatrezor, Pg 13 ©WILDLIFE GmbH/Alamy Stock Photo, ©abadonian, ©fotomarekka, Pg 14 ©PhotoAlto/Alamy Stock Photo, Pg 15 ©galdzer, ©lenanet, ©heibaihui, Pg 16 ©By fish1715, Pg 17 ©Arco Images GmbH/Alamy Stock Photo, ©Nobuo Matsumura/Alamy Stock Photo, Pg 18 ©animatedfunk, ©GlobalP, Pg 19 ©Edwin Remsberg/Alamy Stock Photo, ©By Crystal Eye Studio, Pg 20 ©JasonOndreicka, ©MarsBars, Pg 21 ©rpbirdman, ©kimmycat68, Pg 22 ©xjbxjhxm, Pg 23 ©Artsanova, Pg 24 ©mgfoto, Pg 25 ©Russotwins/Alamy Stock Photo, Pg 26 ©Greentellect_Studio, ©ApisitWilaijit, Pg 27 ©Atelopus, Pg 28 ©arlindo71, ©ranplett, ©doug4537, Pg 29 ©perets, ©PetrP, ©Yakovliev, Pg 30 ©Ljupco,

Edited by: Keli Sipperley
Cover and interior design by: Kathy Walsh

Library of Congress PCN Data

Bugs / Grace Ramsey
(Weird, True Facts)
ISBN 978-1-64156-490-8 (hard cover)
ISBN 978-1-64156-616-2 (soft cover)
ISBN 978-1-64156-728-2 (e-Book)
Library of Congress Control Number: 2018930708

Rourke Educational Media
Printed in the United States of America,
North Mankato, Minnesota